Francis L. Cope Jr.
1925.

The Hibbert Lectures, 1924

THE CHALLENGE OF LIFE

L. P. JACKS, D.D., LL.D., D.Litt.

By L. P. JACKS, D.D., LL.D., D.Litt.

THE CHALLENGE OF LIFE
THE LOST RADIANCE OF THE
   CHRISTIAN RELIGION
A LIVING UNIVERSE
REALITIES AND SHAMS
RELIGIOUS PERPLEXITIES
THE LEGENDS OF SMOKEOVER

THE CHALLENGE OF LIFE

Three Lectures

BY

L. P. JACKS, D.D., LL.D., D.LITT.
PRINCIPAL OF MANCHESTER COLLEGE, OXFORD

"Quit You Like Men"

NEW YORK
GEORGE H. DORAN COMPANY

COPYRIGHT, 1925,
BY GEORGE H. DORAN COMPANY

THE CHALLENGE OF LIFE
— A —
PRINTED IN THE UNITED STATES OF AMERICA

FOREWORD

THESE Hibbert lectures have had a chequered history. They were first delivered as two lectures in Cardiff, Bristol, Southampton and Reading, but differently in each place, according to the nature of the audience. I then went to the United States, and, my mind being full of the subject, I redistributed the matter and enlarged upon it, giving much of it as the Swarthmore Lectures in Harvard University, and then repeating what I found suitable in many other places, both in the East and the Middle West, finally winding up with "The Ethic of Workmanship" at the "commencement" ceremonies of McGill University, Montreal. When the time came for publishing the original lectures, according to my agreement with the Hibbert Trustees, they had become so dispersed that there was nothing for it but to rewrite them from beginning to end. This I have done, without departing, I hope, too far from the original.

The last lecture, on "The Ethic of Workmanship," parts of which were embedded in the original two, and the gist of which was given in Montreal, was subsequently expanded into a lecture to the "Conference for Work Directors, Managers, Foremen and Forewomen," held at Balliol College, Oxford, on September 28, 1924, and then published in the *Hibbert Journal* for October.

L. P. J.

CONTENTS

CHAPTER		PAGE
I:	THE CHALLENGE TO THE INDIVIDUAL	11
II:	THE CHALLENGE TO SOCIETY	47
III:	THE CHALLENGE TO LABOUR (THE ETHIC OF WORKMANSHIP)	79

I: The Challenge to the Individual

I: The Challenge to the Individual

THE alleviation of misery stands for all time among the noblest objects of human endeavour. But the alleviation of misery, which is good with few qualifications, must not be confused with the *removal of difficulty,* which is not good without many qualifications. That this confusion is frequent cannot be denied. Many a scheme which begins with the object of alleviating misery ends, without the promoters being aware of the disastrous change that has taken place, as a scheme for the removal of difficulty. A case in point is that of a public dole intended to alleviate the miseries of unemployment which becomes in practice a means to relieving the worker from the difficulty of finding work and from the trouble of doing it when found.

The amount of misery in the world is so great, and much so clearly undeserved, that the alleviation of it seems to many persons the only object that really matters. No error could be more pardonable; but an error most assuredly it is. Experience has proved that, except it forms part in a much larger and more positive plan of operation, the alleviation of human misery is never effective as a social policy, and may even defeat its own object. A society of which the best that could be said is that all its miseries have been relieved would not be an inspiring spectacle. Conceivably it might be the reverse. A paradox would result. For, if that were the best that could be said, a new misery greater than any from which our supposed society had gained relief would have fallen upon it—that, namely, of having nothing really worth while to do, a condition of insufferable boredom. Man, we may rest assured, was not introduced upon this planet for the sole purpose of not being miserable. Proofs of human progress which prove merely that man is advancing towards a non-miserable existence prove nothing to the point.

While fully admitting the importance of alleviating human misery and the beauty of a life devoted to that object, I am going to plead for the equal importance, in these days, of providing incentives to the tackling of difficulty. Our preoccupation with the relief of distress which, by itself, is much to our credit, has become so absorbing that the need of providing the incentives aforesaid has almost ceased to have a place in the outlook of the social reformer. Yet without incentives to the tackling of difficulty all attempts to relieve human misery, on the social scale, admirably motived though they be, will come to grief. Many are coming to grief at the present moment on account of that, and more will follow. To this cause may be ascribed, for example, the lamentable decay in the ethic of workmanship, which is exceedingly difficult to practise, but fundamental to the right prosperity of civilisation, a theme on which I shall have more to say hereafter. And in many other directions we may watch the insidious process by which schemes and measures, nobly meant by their authors for the alleviation of misery, are immediately wrested by those for whom they are intended, or by designing practitioners from the outside, into means for the elimination of difficulties, the removal of which leaves the objects of this beneficence more miserable than before. Indeed, the main weakness of social reform, in our time, lies precisely at this point. It fails to provide an adequate incentive to the tackling of difficulty. Extreme instances are not unknown in which the claim has been made, in the name of social reform, that no such incentive is needed. But in that case the reformer can hardly be sincere.

The more we learn of the nature of man and of the universe which gives him lodging, the more evident it becomes that man's business on this planet, his part as an actor in the scheme of things, is *difficult*—easy, no doubt, in many a detail, but difficult in the grand outlines and issues, easy in many an interlude, but difficult in the main plot of the drama and in the concatenation of the acts, of which the last is death. Children play on the fringes of it, but child's play is not the business in hand. Nor does the plot grow easier as it thickens, and advances to the point where the last enemy lies ambushed. At every stage of the advance there is a deeper urgency in the call to play the man and to make ready for the final encounter. This is no *game* that man is playing. The words of Cromwell, written on the day before the battle of Dunbar, when he was hemmed in by superior forces and in a precarious position, might be taken as a motto for human life in general, for the whole business of man on this planet—"We are upon an engagement very difficult."

Everything of value the human race has achieved since man began his stormy pilgrimage on the earth bears witness to this. Man's history, in respect at least of all that does him credit, is the record of difficulties conquered, and beyond the point to which history carries us back there lies a vastly longer period in which the human race was holding its own, or slowly fighting its way forward against fearful odds. Every step in the advance that man has made has taxed his resources to the uttermost; and it must never be forgotten that the most difficult steps were accomplished before democracy was thought of or the ballot-box invented. To detach himself from his brute ancestors, to invent his earliest tools, to learn the primitive arts, to lay the rough foundations of civilised life and then to carry it on stage by stage to the point it has now reached —these, one and all, represent titanic achievements, which only a race of heroic fibre could have accomplished. What all this has cost in suffering, in courage, in endurance, in ingenuity, in patient wisdom, baffles the imagination to conceive. I doubt if there was ever a point in the history of mankind of which it could be said that the chances of a further advance were, then and there, in man's favour. From the very first he has been "upon an engagement very difficult," in which the odds, humanly considered, were against him.

I see no prospect at all that these conditions will be essentially altered in the future. The form of the difficulty will doubtless change, but the difficulty itself will remain. To the end of the chapter man will have to go on, not only fighting a battle, but fighting a battle against adversaries that seem to overmatch him—David against Goliath of Gath. His doom, or rather his splendid destiny, is to be for ever attempting the seemingly impossible. At this moment, for example, he is being challenged to create international order out of the prevailing chaos. It looks impossible. The omens are unfavourable, the wiseacres are shaking their heads, and the soothsayers are declaring that it cannot be done. It is for man to defy them. The fathers who begat him have many a time done the like.

There is a dream of human progress which makes it to consist in a gradual *easing* of the lot of man, in the gradual lightening of his task, until the last straw of difficulty has been lifted out of his path, the last peril extinguished, the last lee-shore weathered and all smooth sailing for ever afterwards. May it never come true! Man is not made to live under those conditions; the lines on which he is built are far too high and large to fit into them. He will never accommodate himself to an easy life, unless we are to assume that his nature has degenerated in the meantime. Ill adapted for living an easy life, he is well adapted for living a difficult one. It is precisely when his circumstances are easiest that he gives the poorest account of himself, and the best when he is fighting against odds. Never is he more at home in this universe than when he finds himself "upon an engagement very difficult." "It behoves the son of man to suffer many things that he may enter into his glory." Give him a life in which suffering plays no part, and you defraud him at the core of his being. You say to him, "Be a hero no more. Henceforth take your ease; eat, drink and be merry. Be Fortune's darling and a smiling fool." A wise man turns from your offer with loathing.

In easy circumstances man shows only his middling virtues, and often not even these. Both in his mind and in his body he is adapted for big business, for enterprises of great pith and moment, for the acquisition of astonishing arts that seem impossible till he has practised them, for dangerous expeditions into the unknown, for stern and anxious battles with the powers of darkness, for standing up to tremendous shocks, for enduring heartbreaking reverses, for rising up when he has been wounded and beaten to the ground, and for dying, if need be, sword in hand. To a being so splendidly equipped it is no hardship, no cause for whining, when he finds himself "upon an engagement very difficult": he does not complain of his Maker for that. He praises his Maker, and goes into battle singing psalms. "Here am I," he cries, "with my aptitudes and versatilities; yonder is the universe offering me the very problems, the very tasks those apti-

The Challenge to the Individual 19

tudes and versatilities are made to cope with; here am I, Lord, *send me*." To see man as he truly is, to see the great virtues of which he is capable, to see the ends for which he was created, we must catch him in one of these moments when he is grappling with problems that seem insoluble, when he is addressing himself to tasks that seem beyond his courage and his wit.

The idea that we have a *right* to an easy existence, that life *ought* not to be difficult; that so far as it is difficult we suffer wrong and have a grievance; that the path of progress, therefore, lies in the direction of making things easy all round—this idea lies deeply embedded in the thought of our time. It has become so involved in what is known as our "outlook on life" that we hardly notice its presence, and are unconscious of the extent to which it dominates our minds.

We become conscious of it when we compare modern literature with ancient. Most ancient literatures are heroic in some degree; all literature is so to begin with. Literature begins with the attempt to delineate the mighty deeds of man and to commemorate them for the imitation of posterity. In the earliest written books we hear the echoes of his primitive but tremendous struggle against nature and the wild beasts, in which the odds were so fearfully against him, but in which he came so bravely off. At that stage literature is the story of man's attack upon great difficulties, the story of his wrestle with an angel, sometimes conceived under the dark form of fate or destiny, sometimes as a friendly yet still formidable opponent. The poems of Homer and the great sagas of the North are essentially of this type. They represent the first form of human history, untrue in the sense that the detail is legendary, but profoundly true in the reflection given of the conditions man had to face in breaking out from his brutish entanglement and achieving the first steps towards civilisation. The immense difficulty of the achievement is rightly conceived and never lost sight of.

Nor is there any suggestion in these literatures that life will be easier for those who come after. The conditions will continue the same; the part played by the hero is the part that all men must gird themselves to play; it is by fostering his spirit and confronting our task as he

The Challenge to the Individual

confronted his that we may hope to win through and inherit the kingdoms prepared for us. We are not intended to admire him only, to say, "How noble, how splendid," but to do the like—nay, to *outdo* what has been done. Untiring resourcefulness, inexhaustible patience, invincible valour, indifference to wounds, loyalty to the end—these are the qualities on which man must rely at every stage of his progress to carry him forward to the next. There is no walkover in store for man. He must fight his way forward, as his fathers did before him, and then fight to hold the ground he has won; for the gods, who are wiser than men, have ordained it so. To ask for an easier lot is to show ourselves unworthy of the heroes who begat us, to build habitations of lath and plaster on the foundations they laid in granite. This it was that they encountered; this it is that we must expect and learn to rejoice in. The heroic literatures are not gloomy and grim; they ring with joy, but with a joy that has its roots in valour and is often extracted from pain, the joy of the strong man armed.

"Wilt thou do the deed and repent it, thou hadst better never been born;

Wilt thou do the deed and exalt it; then thy fame shall be outworn;
Thou shalt do the deed and abide it, and set thy throne on high,
And look on to-day and to-morrow as those that never die." [1]

Between the Christian Scriptures and the literature I have just named there are, of course, immense differences of ethical and religious value. And yet, beneath the differences, there is a resemblance well worth noting. In the grand outlines of it the Bible belongs to the heroic age of the world's literature. Never is the Bible interpreted in a sense further removed from the original than when it is taken as pointing mankind to a safe and easy life. The salvation it promises has to be worked out, at every stage, with the fear and trembling proper to the brave man who has measured the perilous nature of the undertaking before him, and *knows* that he is "upon an engagement very difficult." Nor are the difficulties at an end when salvation has been *won*. It has still to be *kept;* and those only can keep it who are able to "stand fast" in an exposed and dangerous position. There is no promise, that I can find, of a time when religion will be "accommodated"

[1] *The Story of Sigurd,* by William Morris.

The Challenge to the Individual

to science or to social aspirations, or to the general demand for smooth-flowing enjoyment, when all its paradoxes will be done away in a reconciliation of everything with everything else, and nothing will be asked of the believer beyond a tame acceptance of the "solutions" provided by experts to the various problems involved; a time, in short, when belief will be easy and salvation can be had for the asking by anybody who has received a good elementary education. This ideal, to which some of our modernist reformers seem to have engaged themselves, has no place in the Bible, neither in the Old Testament nor in the New. "I believe because it is impossible" is certainly not a motto in the spirit of the Bible; it overstates an important truth; and yet between it and the contrary of it, "I believe because it is *easy*," there can be no question which brings us nearer to the Bible. Religion in the Bible is presented as a highly critical affair, as a challenge addressed to the valiant soul, and which none but he can successfully meet.

"The present crisis in religion," so extensively exploited in these days as though it were a phenomenon peculiar to them, is never "absent" from the pages of the Bible. If we say that religion is the valiant facing of a crisis which has a perennial root in human life, and will never be absent so long as man is man, we shall be defining religion in the Bible spirit. "See," says the Deuteronomist, "I have set before thee this day life and death: therefore choose life, that thou and thy seed may live." "Narrow is the gate and straitened the way," says Jesus, "that leadeth to life, and few there be that find it." "Quit you like men," says St. Paul. The choice between life and death has to be *made;* it is, under any conceivable circumstances, a hard choice to make. It will be no easier when "the present crisis in religion" has passed away than it is now. Nor will the narrow road that leads to life be any broader, nor the broad road that leads to destruction any narrower, when religion and science have come to terms, than they were before; nor will there be one occasion the less in human experience when "Quit you like men" is the order of the day. Then, as now, the man who would live a good life, or a religious one, will find himself "upon an engagement very difficult." The Bible holds out no prospect whatsoever of a time when religion

The Challenge to the Individual

will have become a walkover, but warns us, in language whose meaning is unmistakable, to gird up our loins for running a race that will challenge our strength to the uttermost. "They that wait on the Lord," says Isaiah, in words that echo the heroic spirit, "shall renew their strength; they shall mount up with wings as eagles; they shall run and not faint": or, as Brynhild says to Sigurd, they

> "shall set their throne on high,
> And look on to-day and to-morrow as those that never die."

A difficult position to win: a difficult position to hold.

On this ground, and it is the deepest, the claim stands justified that the Bible, in the grand outlines of it, belongs to the heroic literatures of the world. But this is not the only ground. There are many others.

Reading the Synoptic Gospels, for example, trying to read them as they were intended to be received, and dismissing from the mind, as far as I can, the mists of subsequent theorising which obscure their original motives, I find myself in the heroic atmosphere throughout. It is the *deeds* of the central Figure on which they focus the attention, the sayings, or "teachings" as we call them, growing out of the deeds, and not vice versa, which is one of the strongest characteristics of heroic literature. Unfortunately for the right understanding of the Gospels the modern habit of interpretation has reversed this order, insisting that the teaching comes first, and treating the "mighty works" as secondary and, perhaps, not indispensable adjuncts; "illustrations," so to speak; pictures illuminating the text; with the result that we take the Gospel as a *sermon,* which is what it was never intended to be, and lose the force of its impact as a *story,* which is what it originally was. As in all heroic literatures so, in the Gospels, the functions of Hero and Teacher are not discriminated, as we have learnt to discriminate them in modern times. The Hero teaches primarily by what he is and dies, what he *says* being always subordinate to *that* and growing out of it. "The works that I do, these are they that testify of me."

In reversing this method we are, no doubt, taking the line which the modern mind usually follows and believes to be most edifying. But there are dangers in it. Of which the chief is

The Challenge to the Individual 27

this, that we suppose the business of the Gospel can be done by the mere *statement* of ideals extracted from it, such as the Fatherhood of God and the Brotherhood of Man, and come to rely on the statement of these and such-like truths, constantly repeated and enlarged upon, as the force that is to change men's characters and improve their conduct. This is one of the great delusions of our time, to which not a few of our failures and miseries are to be justly ascribed. The truth is rather that every ideal begins to lose its force as an actuating principle from the moment it is turned into a literary property or mere topic for discourse—the real meaning of Carlyle's doctrine of "silence," which has been so much misunderstood.

About all this the late Professor W. P. Ker, in his admirable book on Epic and Romance, has some wise remarks. "An ideal defined or described in set terms is an ideal without any responsibility and without any privilege. It may be picked up and traded on by any fool or hypocrite. Undefined and undivulged it belongs only to those who have some original strength of imagination or will, and with them it cannot go wrong. But a definite ideal, and the terms of its definition may belong to anyone and be put to any use."[1] In the best period of heroic literature the ideal, he goes on to say, though present and active everywhere in the recorded deed, is undefined. It is only when decay sets in that the ideal begins "to walk about as an independent personage."

Among the characteristics of heroic literature to be gathered from Professor Ker's analysis are the following: The hero is always the man who is best at the things with which everyone is familiar; he does not live, after the manner of an aristocrat, in a world of his own elevated above the common level. He lives on the same level as others; does the actions that belong to it; shares the everyday interests of his neighbours; plays the part which all men have to play. But he infuses all this with a nobler quality—"in the world," one might say, "but not of it." He looks after his own affairs, is a good judge of cattle and sails his own ship. He does not expect to be waited on hand and foot. His dignity is not impaired by participating in manual labours nor by "riding in a cart"

[1] *Epic and Romance*, pp. 7-9.

The Challenge to the Individual

like a common churl. He has around him a body of companions, whom he dominates by his personal force, but without attempting to govern them by any system of discipline. He and they form an "order" without rules, none for him and none for them, held together by the nature of the enterprise in which all are engaged and by the temper which the hero throws into it. He takes part with them and allows them to take part with him: his superiority *over* the others involving no sacrifice of his equality *with* them, but having its roots precisely in that. The motives of action are positive, sensible and above-board; there are no secret orders and no elaborate policies. Dignity is obtained by the force of imagination applied to common things, and not by flights into the realm of the sublime. There is no dressing up of ideas to play the part of characters. If the characters are not men, they are nothing; and they all cease talking when they have nothing to do. The deeds exhibited are never large public operations, or the actions of men in the mass; they are always the single deeds of individual persons. Corporations have no part in heroic narrative, but community of interest has, the greatness of the hero being grounded throughout on that which he has in common with those less distinguished than himself. He is the "shepherd of the people." [1]

There is much in the Bible that tallies closely with this description, and the points of resemblance to the Gospels (not mentioned by Professor Ker) will be obvious at a glance. The impact of the Gospels is greatest precisely at those points where the recorded fact is left to speak for itself; least where subsequent moralisings have been allowed to intrude into the original narrative. In the elemental world to which the Gospels belong the "deed" takes precedence of the "word." Graduation as a prophet of the ideal consists in the process of actually laying down one's life, stage by stage, as a ransom for many. In the sophisticated world into which we have been born we graduate in the school of the prophets by our skill in repeating and enlarging on the formula that "we die to live." There is a profound difference between the two things.

"Every parable," says Thoreau, "has a moral.

[1] In this paragraph I have partly quoted and party paraphrased. See *Epic and Romance*, p. 233.

But the innocent enjoy the story." The Gospels were intended for innocent people of the type contemplated by Thoreau, and it is very difficult for those whose theoretical preoccupations have destroyed their innocence, which is an heroic quality, to read them aright. "Except ye become as little children, ye shall in no wise enter the Kingdom of God." And here, too, it should be noted, the saying is not launched into the void and left suspended there as a book maxim, or statement of a general principle, but accompanied both before and after by appropriate actions which embody it. First He sets a little child in their midst, and then, having said what He has to say, lifts it up in His arms and blesses it; which accords very beautifully with Professor Ker's characterisation of the hero as one who "cannot go on talking unless he has something to do."

It is in keeping with all this that ease and leisure are not to be found among the good things which the Bible promises to the faithful. "Tremble, ye women that are at ease," cries Ezekiel; "woe to them that are at ease in Zion," cries Amos; and in the Gospel "take your ease" is the motto of the fool. To the faithful good things are promised in abundance, but always such good things as the valiant soul finds desirable, and never such as please the fool or the coward. *Life* is offered as the certain reward, but always a life of hard fighting, strenuous labour, cross-bearing and pain, with the prospect ahead of the approaching night when no man can work. These are the conditions the faithful soul must count on and be prepared for, not miserably and with a downcast heart, but cheerfully, as one who sees that by embracing them he will find the employment his high nature demands and go on to the fulfilment of his joy.

Nowhere in the Gospels do I find the faintest indication of a "good time coming," either for the individual or the race, when, by the adoption of an appropriate "system" (either of Theology or of Economics), cross-bearing will be done away and lotus-eating take its place; when something will be given for nothing; when the needs of man will be satisfied with four hours' works a day, so that he may be "happy" for the rest of it, with money in his purse to make all smooth. Nowhere do I find the Kingdom of Heaven represented as a state that can

The Challenge to the Individual 37

is not demonstrable by positive proof, it is nevertheless beset with *fewer difficulties* than its opposite, and reasonable on that account. This does not mean, indeed, that life on the whole will be easier for a believer in God than for an unbeliever—that would be bribery and corruption too flagrant even for apologetics at their worst. It refers, of course, to the intellectual side of the matter. But even in that limited reference is it true? Had an inhabitant of London in the days of Queen Elizabeth drawn a detailed picture of London as it exists to-day, would it not then have seemed more "reasonable" to put him in a madhouse than to leave him at large? Had wireless telegraphy been described a hundred years ago, would not the hypothesis that the speaker was talking nonsense have been "attended with less difficulty" than the opposite? "All things," we are told, "are possible to God," and perhaps one of the possibilities included in the saying is that of existing in spite of His non-existence seeming "the more reasonable hypothesis." That certainly was once true of the Hertzian waves. At all events we are on firm ground in saying that the existence of God has nothing whatever to do with its being the *easier* of two hypotheses. If ease and difficulty are to be the test—and they are a poor one under any circumstances—the more difficult of the two hypotheses is, in this case, the more likely to be in accordance with the fact—for the obvious reason that a right conception of God must always be the conception of a Being who is *difficult to believe in,* and to keep on believing in.

On the score of ease and difficulty there is, in sober truth, little to choose between the hypothesis of God's existence and its contrary. Both are immensely difficult. Even if the affirmative hypothesis has a trifle of "ease" to its credit, it does not amount to much; the immense difficulty of belief in God still remains —remains to discourage the timid and feeble, but to assure the valiant that he is on the right track—the strait and narrow road that leads to life. It is at this point that our current apologetics, playing for safety and shunning every position that makes the least call on the heroic spirit, give so lame and feeble an account of the matter. They render the conception of God less worth holding in exact proportion as they make it out "easier" to hold. This is the standing danger of all apologetics. They tend to cheapen their object by the very means they take to render it credible. They have no place in heroic literature, but should rather be considered as the antithesis of it. An age in which apologetic literature accumulates is invariably one in which heroic literature, and the power of understanding it, decay.

For this reason we need to be on our guard when the business on hand is that of accommodating religion to science. Religious belief makes a demand on the heroic spirit. Scientific belief does not. Whence the danger lest, in bringing religious belief to the form in which science can smile upon it, we kill the nerve of religion itself. It is possible for religion to be too deferential to science in this matter. The method of science is not the method of religion, and the attempt to work either in the harness of the other can have but one of two results: either science will cease to be scientific, or religion will cease to be religious.

Of course there will be many who say that a belief has no credentials unless it can be made to work in scientific harness. And that is strictly true if "working" is taken to mean the *controllable* working of a machine. But there is another kind of working which is not that of a harnessed machine, but of the unharnessed wind, blowing "where it listeth, and thou hearest the sound thereof, but cannot tell whence it cometh nor whither it goeth"; and there can be little doubt that amid the sum-total of the powers that have moulded, and are still moulding, the destinies of man, the "working" of the wind plays a greater part than the working of the machine. One day, perhaps, the known winds will be catalogued, captured and harnessed to the yoke—this is what the "new psychology" is now attempting. But what of the winds that are unknown? The cave of Æolus has reserves that we know not of. No sooner is one of his messengers captured and tamed than another, liberated by the removal of the first, takes wing and beats boisterously on the four corners of the house. On that road there is no end. It is not with the ideal that "walks about as an independent personage" that the heroic spirit has, primarily, to make his account, but with an ideal that is "undefined and undivulged." When all winds have been tamed there still remains untamed the One who rides on the wings thereof. Him no man can domesticate.

It is therefore with caution and reserve that we should make our approach to the conception of God so prominent in modern theology—the conception of a being whose existence is the solution of a problem, the solvent of an intellectual difficulty, smiled on by science. So far as this conception attracts us by the "ease" it seems to offer, as the satisfaction of a desire to be "comfortable" on the ease-loving side of our nature, it is leading us, not towards religion, but away from it. Thus regarded it falls into one class with the ethic that plays for safety, with the social reform which constructs the millennium in terms of four hours' work a day and the rest leisure, and with the sentimentalism which aims at making all men "happy" in the sense that their interests are automatically secured by a "system" and the highest part of their nature thrown out of employment—all dwelling together "at ease in Zion." Equipped by social reform with the conditions of a perfectly safe existence, made "happy" in the sense that lotus-eating has taken the place of cross-bearing, furnished by morals with a formula of safe-conduct through all dangerous places and by theology with a smooth-turning key to the enigmas of the universe, man would have lost everything which gives value and dignity to his existence on this planet.

Man was not made for a "comfortable" existence, and is only belittled by attempts to satisfy him on those lines. Whether we study the structure of his body or the structure of his mind, we see him designed for difficult and majestic operations, and as one who will never be satisfied with anything that deprives him of these.

I see, then, no reason to believe that the Kingdom of Heaven will take the form of a "soft job," either for the race at large or for the individual members of it. The universe is not planned to that end, and those men and nations that act as though it were, will unquestionably get the worst of it in the long run. That delusion, which has wrought havoc with the civilisations of the past, will be our undoing also if we are foolish enough to indulge it.

The Challenge to the Individual 43

Dr. Foakes-Jackson, in a recent book,[1] has called much-needed attention to a feature in the life of the Early Church which illustrates what I have said. Civil life in those days was safe and tranquil; those who wanted "ease and happiness" could have it. But there was one danger-spot—the Christian Church: join that and you took your risk of being thrown to the lions. To that very fact, thinks Dr. Foakes-Jackson, may be traced, in no small measure, the astonishing growth of the Church in those centuries. *The Church became a centre of attraction for heroic souls,* and as such conquered the world of that day. On what other terms, I would ask, can the Christian Church conquer the world in which we are living now?

[1] "Studies in the Life of the Early Church," p. 119.

II: The Challenge to Society

II: The Challenge to Society

OF all the debts we owe to William Morris, due acknowledgment of which awaits him in the future, perhaps the greatest arises from the version he made of "the Story of Sigurd." So far as it is possible, in these days, to revive the spirit of heroic literature, Morris, in that poem, may be said to have succeeded. The version is far from being literal. But Morris himself, like Scott, was temperamentally in the direct line of descent from the heroes, and their spirit, which is the essential thing, speaks to us authentically in his verse. Morris was a "lonely man," as every hero, in some sense, is.

"The Story of Sigurd" as presented by Morris tells, in the finest part, of the education of a hero by a woman—the education of Sigurd by Brynhild, herself heroic. It will be found, if the matter be inquired into, that most of the world's greatest men have been educated by women, at one or other of the critical points of their training, and most of the world's greatest women have earned their title to everlasting honour precisely by educating such men at those critical points, sometimes early in life and sometimes late. Though the modern woman no longer seems to recognise this as one of her functions in the universe, and the highest of them (which goes far, perhaps, to account for the dearth of great men in these times), it is impossible to believe that a function so clearly intended by Nature to be supreme can have fallen into permanent obsolescence. The day for its revival will come, and when it comes "the Story of Sigurd" will be read not only by heroic women, but by male moralists, social reformers and theologians with a greater interest than it has for the present generation.

Embedded in "the Story of Sigurd" lies a conception of the Divine Nature, which, though it is never distinctly formulated—and that is not to be looked for in heroic narratives—is yet intensely operative in the "educational system" applied by Brynhild to the training of the hero. Reading continuously, we gradually come to feel the form and pressure of it, and there is one passage, of two lines only, where it rises very near to the surface:

The Challenge to Society 49

"Love thou the Gods, but withstand them, lest thy fame should fail at the end,
And thou be their thrall and their bondman, who wert born for their very friend."

The idea of these old pagans seems to have been that if we would have the higher powers for our friends we must be ready at times to stand up to them as though they were our foes. "Love thou the gods, but *withstand* them." We are reminded of Emerson's saying about friendship, "Let thy friend be to thee as a beautiful enemy," and of Chesterton's—that we cannot reform the world effectively unless we both hate it and love it. "Son of man, stand upon thy feet and I will speak to thee," is a parallel utterance from the Bible.

The gods are not conceived as making things easy for man, but as making them difficult: their beneficence takes that form. They set him hard tasks, they give him perplexing problems, they match him against superior odds, they send him forth on long and perilous adventures, such as slaying dragons and capturing the treasures they guard, such as rescuing women from the clutches of monsters and abominable tyrants—the hero's return to the woman for the "education" he has received in that quarter. They spread the insoluble before him and say, "Solve *that!*" They fling the impossible at his feet and say, "Do *that!*" They put his body to its mettle, his mind also and his soul. They are the challengers. They take him down into hell as the first stage on his journey to heaven, and salt him with fire. When he finds himself at the crisis of his fate, and all seems to hang upon a hair, let him say to himself, "The god has done it: the god has given me this: it is the work of my beautiful enemy."

From this to the doctrine of the Cross the way is not so long as it seems. Each speaks a language of its own; but the principle is the same. It is a point of contact between Odin and Christ.

Such is the challenge, and the man whom the gods love is the man who stands up to it. If you "withstand" them like a man your enemy proves himself "beautiful"; he becomes your friend at need; is found at your side at the moment when all seems lost; his strength made perfect in your weakness; his shield thrown around you; his right arm laid bare in your defence; he kindles a light for you in the darkness and brings you at last triumphant to Valhalla. But if you fall to complaining and self-pity; if you go after your own "ease" and "happiness"; if you hire a substitute to fight your battle or to carry your load, the beauty of your enemy shall never be seen by you. He will remain your enemy with a vengeance; he will give you misery and dishonour; he will make you a slave and a thrall; he will be ashamed of you—of you who were born for his "very friend"; you shall be slain at the end like a dog, your carcase shall be cast out to the wild beasts and you never shall be any more. A drastic doctrine surely! But not without its analogue elsewhere. "Of him shall the Son of Man be *ashamed*." "Depart, ye cursed, into the æonian fire prepared for the devil and his angels."

In all this I find matter of profound significance and high value, which the modern world has lost sight of, but which was never more needed than it is in these days, with their doctrine of God as the "solvent of difficulties" and their ideal, yet more debased, of "ease and happiness" as the goal of human progress. The challenge of life has not ceased to call us, and there are no signs whatever that the terms of it will be relaxed. Our "beautiful enemy," who knows what is good for us better than we do, has ordained it so.

At no stage of man's history has it ever been easy to bring his life to a victorious issue. The good life, says Aristotle, is, by its nature, a difficult affair. But far more difficult for us than it was for the Greeks of Aristotle's time. The principles of the good life are, no doubt, the same now as they were then, the same yesterday, to-day and for ever; but the increasing complexity of the social organism has enormously increased the difficulty of their *right application* and the range of the danger that has to be run from fools, knaves and hypocrites who misapply them, either through ignorance or subtlety. If science has removed one set of difficulties it has also furnished us with the means to create others far greater —means we are not slow to use. And, while science widens the range of the challenge, education gives it a sharper point, by opening our eyes to unsuspected evils and by making us more sensitive to those we knew of before.

The standards have risen, and the social facts to which we must apply them have increased in range, in complexity, in mass and in acquired momentum—this last especially. Our responsibilities have multiplied; our tasks, both personal and social, have grown more onerous and more delicate. When was the life of nations such a turmoil of unbridled forces as it is to-day? When were the problems of civilisation so numerous and so perplexing? When was statesmanship so difficult? When was order so necessary and yet so hard to achieve? Who can doubt that the Challenge of Life, in changing its form, has only taken on a deeper note? And what if human progress should turn out to be nothing else than a joint operation of these two things—the deepening of the challenge that comes from above and the growing alacrity of the response that comes from below? Be that as it may, of one thing we may be sure. Human progress does *not* consist in a gradual removal of the Challenge of Life. On that road there is nothing to be expected but misery and defeat, the decay of manhood, the death of the arts and the downfall of civilisation. It is the broad road that leads to destruction, and many there be that take it, both men and nations.

Once more there is nothing in this to complain of or to pull a long face over. Our "beautiful enemy" knew what he was about when he ordained it thus. If our difficulties are immense, immense also are our resources for coping with them. Our measure was taken first, and a task then assigned which men such as we, with spiritual forces waiting to befriend us if we stand to it manfully, can most assuredly accomplish. To each man, to each age according to his several ability. The ability of our age is great. So, too, is our task.

In what has gone before no secret has been made of my belief that between the presentation of the heroic ideal in the literature of paganism, on the one hand, and in the Bible, on the other, there exists a significant affinity. But an equally significant difference has now to be noted.

In the Homeric poems, which are the Epic of Greece, and in the Northern Sagas, which, as William Morris truly insisted, are the Epic of the Anglo-Saxon race, the heroic spirit ex-

The Challenge to Society

presses itself primarily in the form of martial valour. The instrument of its working is the sword, not as wielded by an abstraction called the "State," or "Justice," or "Law," but in the hand of the individual hero. The sword, or some equivalent weapon, with the strength and wisdom of the hero behind it, is almost the object of a cult. It approaches deification in the Volsunga and is named "the Wrath." The wrath of gods, as well as of men, is in it, reflected on its blue and glittering edge.

The Bible never goes as far as this in the glorification of the sword. Nevertheless there are stages in the history of Israel which approach it. In the book of Exodus the "Lord" is expressly celebrated as "a man of war—the Lord is His name." Joshua, Gideon and David are martial heroes. Elijah is the counsellor of warriors; he himself slays the prophets of Baal with the sword, the passage in which the deed is recorded reminding us of many an episode in the Sagas. It is indeed a noteworthy fact that the Bible mentions the sword oftener than any other instrument of human invention—a glance at a concordance will show this. For one reference you will find to the hammer, the axe, the ploughshare, the mill and the loom you will find fifty to the sword. Nor are the references confined to the Old Testament. As at the beginning of the Old a flaming sword keeps guard over the gates of Paradise, so at the end of the New there stands among the golden candlesticks "one like unto a son of man with a sharp two-edged sword proceeding out of his mouth." "I am come," said Jesus, "not to bring peace, but a sword." In St. Paul's account of the Christian warfare it is with "the sword of the spirit" that the believer carves his way, and overthrows the "strongholds" that oppose him. Turned into a metaphor, the sword still remains an *indispensable* metaphor, more frequently used than any other and the most trenchant of them all. At the highest level of New Testament religion there is something that the sword alone can express.

Yet the change from the literal to the metaphorical usage is profoundly significant. Here the Bible conception of the heroic life goes far beyond the point reached by the epics of the Greeks and of the Goths, and the difference I spoke of a moment ago makes a decisive appearance. Beginning, as they did, with a conception of the heroic life as typified in the fact that "there were in Israel eight hundred thousand valiant men who drew the sword" the Bible sublimated the type until it reached the point which modern hymnody has reproduced (with flamboyant additions, not true to the original), in "Onward, Christian soldiers, marching as to war." The Bible sublimated the type, but retained its essential quality. Righteousness became the object of heroic endeavour; not righteousness as attainable by the *via negativa* of safe-conduct, but heroic righteousness to be won and kept, even to the point of "resisting unto blood," by the self-same indomitable valour which had made the spear and bow victorious when Israel was a marching host—a note finely echoed by Milton in many a resonant passage of *Samson Agonistes:*

> "Oh, how comely 'tis and how reviving
> To the spirits of just men long oppressed,
> When God into the hands of their deliverer
> Puts invincible might
> To quell the mighty of the earth .
> He all their ammunition
> And feats of war defeats,
> With plain heroick magnitude of mind
> And celestial vigour arm'd."

And again:

> "But he, though blind of sight,
>   Despised, and thought extinguisht quite,
>   With inward eyes illuminated,
>   His fiery virtue roused
>   From under ashes into sudden flame;
>   And as an evening dragon came,
>   Assailant on the perchèd roosts
>   And nests in order ranged
>   Of tame villatic fowl; but as an eagle
>   His cloudless thunder bolted on their heads."

Such was the sublimation achieved by the Old Testament, to be carried yet further in the New, until it became almost lyrical in St. Paul, bearing about in his body the dying of the Lord Jesus, perplexed, but not unto despair, sore beset, but fainting not. From first to last hard fighting remained the keynote of it, and the order of the day was "Quit you like men." Between "the wrath of the Lamb" and the Wrath that was Sigurd's sword the difference indeed is great. But such is the resemblance beneath them.

At an earlier point in these lectures the remark was offered, which I must now enlarge upon, that corporations play no part in the heroic literatures of the past. The history of

Israel, indeed, presents what looks at first sight an exception to this, an exception apparently so large as to destroy the significance of the statement. In the Deuteronomist and in the greater prophets Israel is conceived as corporately responsible to God, as corporately rewarded or punished, and the indications are that this mode of thought had a very early root in the life of the nation. But a closer examination shows a wide difference between this and the idea of corporate responsibility as we now attach it to the action of organised groups. The righteousness or iniquity of Israel, for which it is rewarded or punished, is the totalised effect of the right or wrong actions of the individual members in the conduct of their daily lives, and sometimes, as in the case of Saul and of David, it follows on the consequence of actions performed by the leader for the time being. The nation is righteous when righteous men are in the majority and have the upper hand, wicked under the contrary condition; in either case a collection of acting units, rather than itself the acting unit and responsible as such. The conception of "society" acting as an organised whole, of the "social mind" or "social will" as capable of initiating action and carrying it through, had not yet arisen; those who read the history of Israel in these terms are reading into it the thought of a much later or a different age. So too the armies that fought under the walls of Troy are collections of heroes, each relying mainly on the strength of his own right arm—a very different thing from the drilled and regimented masses which the word "army" suggests to the modern mind. The deeds recorded are the deeds of these individuals, not summary or public operations, not the deeds of men in the mass previously agreed upon by majority voting or otherwise brought to a unitary issue.

No doubt in all this the writers of the Old Testament were on the way to the more developed conception of corporate responsibility, but the conception as it stands is undeveloped, and not at variance with the characteristics of epic literature in general. In the later books of the New Testament the idea of a multitude acting as a unit does indeed make a first appearance under the form of the Church, but the conception is floating and unfixed. In Thucydides, Plato and Aristotle we find it, of course, more fully formed. But Thucydides, Plato and Aristotle are post-heroic; almost as far removed from Homer, in spirit if not in time, as we are from the Sagas—when "the healthy knew not of their health, but only the sick."

But now, to a degree unknown in earlier and simpler societies, the fortunes of civilisation for weal or woe have come to depend on vast concerted operations, on organised mass action, on the action of State upon State, of Church upon Church, of party upon party, of class upon class, of group upon group, on the interaction of all these one with another, on the reciprocal impact of multitudes in their organised totalities, under whatever policy they may severally be pursuing. Mass action, of course, was not unknown in primitive society; we have it in the siege of Troy, the fight at Finnesburgh, the burning of the house of Njal. But mass action, then, was confined almost exclusively to the operations of war, nor were the interacting masses comparable either in magnitude or in the variety of their groupings to those which now interact not in war only, but in many other fields, of which the economic is the chief, where the vital interests of millions of human beings are at stake. Nor is the action of these enormous masses on one another to be understood as the mere sum-total of the actions of the individual units composing the mass, a condition more nearly approached when the mass is small (as in the Greek city State), though even there not fully reached. As mass action it has qualities of its own entirely diffcrent from those belonging to the actions of the component units, and the difference increases with the increase of the mass. The individual units might all be heroes, but the mass action cowardly—like "an army of lions commanded by asses" which receives orders to retreat at the moment when victory lies within its grasp—an humiliation not unknown in the Great War, and which more than one gallant nation has had to endure from its elected government in the affairs of peace.

The enormous increase the modern world has witnessed both in the range and variety of mass action is mainly due to the advance of democracy, to the permeation by the democratic spirit of all human undertakings both political, economic and religious. In almost every department of life we see the actions of the individual moral agent becoming more and more subordinated to action of the group to which he belongs and of which he is a voting member, and I suppose that socialism would be the culmination of this process.

But while democracy has thus promoted mass action in all directions, it has failed to produce the morality by which mass action is to be governed. This failure becomes more pronounced as we proceed from the lesser masses to the greater, until it becomes almost total on the field of international relations, where the interacting masses are the nations of the earth. Except of the most inadequate kind international ethic does not exist.

So the world to-day stands in this strange position. On the one hand, the field where a developed consciousness of right and wrong is most vital to the well-being of civilisation is, unquestionably, the field of mass action. On the other, it is on the field of mass action that the distinction between right and wrong is least developed and most obscure.

It would appear, then, that democracy **in**

"solving the problem of government"—as many think it has done—has introduced a new and greater problem, which at the moment remains unsolved: that of creating a morality adequate to the situation itself has brought about—a morality of mass action. Who can doubt that democracy, also, is "upon an engagement very difficult"? Its children are out of control.

As to the basis on which the morality of mass action may be founded certain suggestions will be offered later on. At this point it is enough if we ask a question as to the general *level* on which mass morality, the morality which is to govern the relations of peoples, states, Churches, classes and groups, will stand. Will it stand on an inferior and unheroic level, and consist of such principles as can be extracted from the "self-regarding" interests of the masses concerned, enough to secure them in the undisturbed pursuit by each of its own aims, but not enough to unite them in the heroic achievement of a common purpose? Or will it stand on the heroic level where "die to live" may at any moment write itself across the face of the heavens and challenge acceptance by this "mass" or by that, by this nation or by that, as the order of the day?

For my own part I cannot hesitate as to the answer, strange as it needs must sound in the ears of many. *The morality of mass action must be the highest morality known to man— that is, the morality of the hero.* It must be that or it will fail of its purpose and come to nothing.

In the epic literature of the past, "corporations," as we have seen, play no part. In the epic of the future, if such a thing is to be, a great part and a noble will be theirs. That part has yet to be created. If not created and not acted upon, the downfall of Western civilisation is assured.

This task the higher powers—give them what name you will—have assigned to our age and generation. They are challenging men, now, by whole societies, by states, by Churches, by classes, by groups, by whatever form of incorporation man has achieved. They are not forbearing—as their manner is—to put us on our mettle, to give us that to do which demands the mobilisation of wisdom, courage and energy, to the uttermost of our resources, in Church and State, in school and laboratory. They are flinging the impossible at the feet of these groupings, and saying to them, jointly and singly, "Do *that*—or perish from off the face of the earth!" On vested interests that dare not put themselves to the hazard; on groups that have rights, but no duties; on "systems" that make things *easy* all round; on institutions that play for safety; on democracies that put their trust in majority voting, these high Challengers smile not. Their friendship (through which alone the impossible gets itself *done*) is reserved for a very different kind of enterprise. It was so when Jesus warned the disciple who would save his life that most assuredly he would lose it; it was so when Brynhild "spake wisely" in the ear of Sigurd. Then the Word was to individuals; but now not to them only, but to every organised multitude that democracy has brought into being, to nations, to society at large. Let democracy pay heed to this:

"When thou hearest the fool rejoicing, and he saith,
  'It is over and past

And the wrong was better than right, and hate turns into love at the last,
And we strove for nothing at all, and the gods are fallen asleep,
For so good is this world a-growing that the evil good shall reap,'
Then loosen thy sword in the scabbard, and settle the helm on thine head,
For men betrayed are mighty, and great are the wrongfully dead." [1]

I have already mentioned a great enterprise, now before the world, which falls into the class of action I am describing—the attempt to create international order out of the prevailing chaos, the attempt to establish a League of Nations. In this the Challenge of Life, as addressed by the Higher Powers to nations *as nations,* and not to individuals only, comes to a spearhead for this age and generation. Without a measure of the heroic spirit, perhaps a large measure, on the part of all the nations concerned in it, and especially of the great nations, this enterprise cannot and will not be brought to a successful accomplishment. The only kind of action that can do this is action on the heroic level—action, that is, in which risk is apparent from the outset and self-

[1] Brynhild in *The Story of Sigurd.*

renunciation imperative all round. A group of nations each playing for its own safety and jointly engaged in devising machinery to protect each one, automatically, from the selfishness of the others represents, not the conditions out of which a League of Nations is likely to arise, but the conditions in which it is flatly impossible. On these terms the "challenge" is not being accepted, but refused; or rather—and this is worse—is being refused under a disguise which formally accepts it, but which the Higher Powers see through and abhor. If it be true, as some have contended, and still contend, that the "State" as such is incapable of self-renunciation, that self-regard is the law of its being, and that heroic action of the type which disregards the "self," or puts it to the hazard, is not therefore to be demanded of the "State"—if this be true let an end be put at once to an enterprise clearly founded on the principle of "dying to live." Either the League of Nations is an heroic enterprise or it is nothing—or, still worse, nothing disguised as something. The right attitude of the State to this enterprise is well defined in the counsel of Brynhild to Sigurd. With ears stopped to "the

The Challenge to Society

fool rejoicing," let him "loosen his sword in the scabbard, and settle the helm on his head." And there are many other enterprises, to be accomplished by mass action, of which the same might be said. Education is one of them —let the mention of it suffice.

Believing, then, that the Challenge of Life to our generation is primarily for *group action on the heroic level*—impossible, of course, if the individuals composing the group are unheroic —I have to confess that the signs of the times, so far as I can read them, do not indicate that the Challenge is being *met,* or even that the willingness to meet it exists. Of group action there is great abundance, more than any previous age has seen or dreamed of as possible; and the forms and varieties of it are endless. Leaving war aside as a debatable exception, they are all of the self-regarding or unheroic type. Governments, Trades Unions, Industrial Trusts are there to protect their own interests, vested for the most part, or the interests of those they represent, to protect them if need be at the expense of other interests, but to protect them first and foremost. Nor can it be claimed that the Churches form an exception.

The chaos of modern life is the chaos of self-protectionism, in which the efforts put forth by innumerable groups, each to protect itself, renders the whole structure of civilisation, on which their fortunes are embarked together, radically insecure, and leaves it without unitary guidance, drifting no man knows whither. The unheroic character of the total enterprise is the outstanding feature of it. That this is what the "beautiful enemy" expects of civilisation can hardly be thought of as probable. Surely the Son of Man is *ashamed* of it all.

The conclusion is confirmed when we turn to the social literature of our time—the literature in which novelists and playwrights record their impressions, reformers outline their plans and their systems and (it must be added) social quacks advertise their cure-alls, this last being the most extensive department.

Throughout the whole of this literature two conceptions, two modes of thought will be found running, and sometimes strangely intermingled.

The first is the notion that the challenge of life which society has to meet in these days consists of a series of "problems," each of which

The Challenge to Society 71

will be adequately dealt with when it has received a "solution" from the appropriate expert. The hope is held out that by the comparatively easy method of rightly stating the "problem" and producing the "solution," society will be able to extricate itself from that "engagement very difficult" in which it is now being put to the test. That this method—the method of problem-and-solution—is by itself a somewhat feeble answer to the challenge will hardly be doubted. An examination of the various solutions offered will increase the doubt by revealing this significant fact: that not one of them would attain the object in view unless it were backed up by an heroic spirit of self-renunciation in the groups to whose action it refers. We find a typical example of this in the "solution of the social problem" offered by the Eugenists—again let the mention of it suffice.

Along with the method of problem-and-solution, and mingling with it, goes the method of disease-and-remedy. The first appeals to us on the intellectual side, the second on the philanthropic. The word "remedy"—and what word is more prominent in social discussion—has strong attractions for the philanthropist, intent on alleviating the miseries of mankind. The quest for "remedies" is felt to be a worthy occupation for good men. So it is, provided the evil we are coping with is really *sickness,* and not something else. But repeated often, repeated in all connexions and issues, "remedy" acquires a sinister sound at which even philanthropy might shudder. So repeated, it carries the suggestion that the social organism is *radically diseased,* that society is falling into the doctor's hands, and is coming to think of itself—if society can be said to think—as an *invalid.*

Once let that idea, and the sick fancies attendant upon it, get possession of the social mind and the last hope may be abandoned of raising mass action to the heroic level. Society, convinced of its invalid condition, will then behave like the invalid who has wrought himself into that condition with the aid of a clinical thermometer, a book on domestic medicine and a chemist's shop round the corner—querulous, complaining, quarrelsome, faint-hearted. That society will spend its energies, not in wholesome exercise, honest work and the hard wrestling to which the "beautiful enemy" never fails to challenge it, but in hawking its maladies from one political "cure" to another, and in meeting the ruinous charges which those establishments impose upon the resources of their credulous clients.

And here we encounter that disastrous phenomenon of our times—the *social quack doctor*, whose function it is to exploit the sick fancies of his day and generation, to trade upon bad dreams and low spirits and to poison society with patent medicines. The remedies of orthodox science, indeed, when applied to the maladies of the body politic, are not always sure in their working, and often kill where they are meant to cure; but Heaven protect us all from the social quack! His name is Legion, the field of his operations is illimitable, credulity waits for him everywhere, nor is there any to convict him of incompetence or to call him to account for his villainies. Between him and the genuine reformer the difference is immense, but not always apparent, for there is no "recognised diploma" which the one has and the other has not.

How then shall we know them? By their fruits mainly, which appear unmistakably in the time of harvest. But then, alas, the knowledge comes too late to be of much use. For an earlier test they may be known by this—that while the genuine reformer speaks occasionally of disease-and-remedy, as indeed he must, the quack speaks of nothing else. Of the two, again, the quack contrives for himself the softer nest, feathered by selling cures for poverty, sometimes poisonous, but oftener mere water insidiously flavoured, and all guaranteed to be infallible—a mode of growing rich that reduces the proceedings of Tetzel with his indulgences to a peccadillo in comparison. Our quack, also, is fond of the word "diagnosis," which the genuine reformer avoids, and is prepared, if profit be in sight, to "diagnose" the universe and prescribe the appropriate pill.

All nations that fall into his hands sicken, disintegrate and ultimately perish; to be *governed* by him is, of all social disasters, the most to be dreaded. While posing as a pacifist, and doing a roaring trade in peace-pills, he secretly manœuvres to get the army at his back; this done, his tyranny, than which none is more implacable, becomes absolute; all throats must now swallow his physic or be shot, and no dog may bark, no mouse squeak, without his permission.

The Challenge to Society

Such is the doom in store for societies which fall into the hands of the social quack and learn from him to construe their state in terms of disease-and-remedy. Nothing is more offensive to the Higher Powers. Inevitably, there comes a time when the "beautiful enemy," his long-suffering at an end, changes his beauty for a cloak of vengeance and executes his errand on those miserable societies, armed with the Wrath of the Lamb.

These being the main roads that lead to the extinction of the heroic spirit in society, and to the certain vengeance that follows, is there any other road that gives promise of a more auspicious ending? I think there is at least one, opening out from the very spot where industrial civilisation is now standing, but narrow and straitened, like all the roads that lead to life. I call it the Ethic of Workmanship. This I will attempt to describe in the next lecture, only saying in advance that the Ethic of Workmanship is "an engagement very difficult," having little in common with the method of problem-and-solution, and less with the method of disease-and-remedy, and implacably opposed to the social quack.

III: The Challenge to Labour
(The Ethic of Workmanship)

III: The Challenge to Labour (The Ethic of Workmanship)

THE significance of the question addressed by the rich young ruler who came "running" to Jesus, as well as of the answer given to it, may easily be overlooked through want of emphasis on an important word. The question was, "What shall I *do* to inherit eternal life?" The answer, after the prelude of a few generalities, came sharply to the point. It indicated something definite to be *done;* to be done at once; and it was something very difficult, which none of the previous generalities, weighty as they were, had touched upon. The form of it—and the fact is important—was that of a financial operation; not merely to give his possessions away, but to *sell* them first, presumably for the best price they would justly fetch: sold at any price below this, the poor, who were to receive the proceeds, would obviously be defrauded to that extent.

Whether the young man did as he was told is

not known. It is commonly assumed that he did not, which facilitates moralising, but lowers it. There is no conclusive evidence to settle the question. He went away "sorrowful"; but perhaps it was the natural sorrow of one whose mind was made up to part with his treasures. May not that be the reason why Jesus as He looked upon him "loved him"?

In these days our inquiries about eternal life, or about our spiritual interests in general, are seldom met by definite instructions as to what we must *do*. More frequently they are answered by telling us what we must *think,* and avoid thinking, about God, the universe, and our own nature; for example, that we must think of all these as spiritual and not as material. Even when instructions as to what we should do are given, they are mostly expressed in a general form, as that we should make a practice of being just, merciful and devout, which contrasts sharply with the very precise and peremptory order given to the rich young ruler.

General instructions are, no doubt, unavoidable in the conditions under which the modern teaching of religion and ethics is carried on.

But they have a drawback, which is, that their generality causes them to be forgotten, or at least to lose their force, in the intervals between the time at which they are received and the time when opportunity comes for putting them into practice, which may not be till long afterwards. The time-factor in these high matters is extremely important, though seldom taken account of. An instance occurs to me of a friend of mine who was converted to a very sound philosophy of the universe about three months before he became heir to a considerable property. Had the conversion and the legacy occurred on the same day there is no telling what might have come of it. But in the three months' interval, which was spent in a rest-cure rendered necessary by the mental labours which had brought him into the point of philosophical conversion, my friend's new philosophy lost so much of its force that when the time came for applying it to his legacy he seemed to have forgotten all about it. That a vast amount of general instruction both in religion and morals is constantly being sterilised by similar causes cannot be doubted. It was characteristic of the method of Jesus to avoid this danger by giving very precise instructions and requiring their execution *on the spot*. He was by no means indifferent to the value of right thinking, but He saw, what few of His followers have seen so clearly, that the first step to right thinking about eternal life is a right action, done decisively and with the least possible delay. Deliberation and discussion are good; but when these are indefinitely protracted the devil gets time to don his disguise as an angel of light and claim the right to give the casting vote. "What thou doest, do quickly" is sometimes a sound maxim in the doing of evil; but oftener in the doing of good.

The ethic of workmanship is an attempt to apply this method to the work of the world as it is carried on in the morally tumultuous civilisation of to-day. Under conditions rendered enormously difficult by the long neglect of it, the ethic of workmanship would concentrate attention on the *thing done* as the hinge on which the spiritual fortunes of mankind must ultimately turn.

Now "the thing done," in industrial society, consists, in the main, of its *daily work,* in the endless variety of occupations, as these would be revealed by taking a bird's-eye view of the roaring activities of some great city, like Manchester or Chicago, or by perusing the "business" section of the Post Office Directory. I say the "business" section rather than the "residential." For though in the "residential" department a thousand things are done daily about which much that is ethically important has to be said, it is where the tall chimneys are smoking, the skyscrapers shutting out the sun, and before the traffic of the main thoroughfares has thinned out into suburban quietudes, that the ethic of workmanship gets the first grip on its task.

Indeed the main difference between a culture founded on the ethic of workmanship and a culture founded on other ethics is indicated precisely in this: that while the latter aims first at the residential suburbs, the former aims first at the financial and industrial centre. It is in the centre, and not in the suburbs, that the thing is *done* which counts most in determining whether Manchester and Chicago shall inherit eternal life or not.

To be sure, the suburbs are mainly occupied by *homes,* many of them models in their kind both outwardly and inwardly; and, outwardly at least, these homes improve in character the farther they are removed from the business centre, the architecture becoming more dignified, the gardens more spacious, and the garden-parties more picturesque. Now all men know what the home contributes towards fashioning the character of a people. But it must not be forgotten, when studying the psychology of Manchester, Chicago, or any other great city, that most of the homes where this fashioning actually goes on are to be found at points much nearer the centre, long before the gardens begin; that many of them are not models in their kind, either outwardly or inwardly, but slums or semi-slums—black spots in the very eye of the city, directly caused by the evils our ethic would combat, and in close proximity to the seat of the mischief. For these and many similar reasons the ethic of workmanship is not to be disturbed in its main principles by anything that may be said about the influence of the home, but persists, as before, in operating from the centre outwards, and not vice versa. The root of the matter is in Market Street, Michigan Avenue, Cheapside and Lower Broadway. In which connexion it may be remarked incidentally that the ethic of workmanship looks with some misgiving at the transference of places of worship from the working to the residential quarter, well understanding the causes of it, but fearing that the result will be seen in a return to the suburban righteousness of the scribes and Pharisees, with its lamentable want of grip on the weightier matters of the law. The closer the neighbourhood of worship and work, the better for both.

Surely it may be accepted as self-evident that so long as civilisation remains predominantly *industrial,* the moral qualities of the peoples engaged in it will be determined in the main by the *quality of their industry,* by the motives that inspire it, by the aims it has in view, by the degree of real value found in the products and services it yields. Between these and the characters of the men and women who carry on the industrial process, in all the variety of its occupations, there will be an inevitable correspondence. If the work is uninspired by the passion for excellence, everything else will show a like deficiency. Expel the passion for excellence from the sphere of *work,* and the room that remains, in industrial society, for the introduction of it elsewhere is reduced to insignificance. All the fine arts, of which righteous living is the chief, will decay. Or, to vary the statement, if the quality of the work to be done be such that it pulls men down in the moral scale, who can devise operations that will prove effective in raising them up? Neither the statesman, the schoolmaster nor the parson. The best we can then devise will be mere make-weights to an evil which, on the whole, is more powerful than they. When all that culture and government can effect is to counteract in the parentheses of life evils inherent in the main texture of it, the schools, the universities, the parliaments and the churches are obviously fighting a losing battle. If "truth, beauty and goodness," or whatever else be the names of the eternal values, are to be effectively at home in a working world, they must be lodged in its *work*. If that is false, little else can be true; if that is ugly, little else can be beautiful; if that is evil, little else can be good. For work, in an industrial community, is at least three-fourths of life—whatever may be said of "conduct"—and there is no prospect that the proportion will diminish.

The ethic of workmanship lays the main stress on the *quality of the work done,* and treats this as the growing-point of the virtues appropriate to industrial civilisation—such as justice, mercy, pity and loving-kindness. The growing-point, but not the ripened product. For our ethic is by no means unconcerned with the question of just and humane relationships between the parties engaged in the work, especially employers and employed. But it does not *begin* by raising that or any similar question. It begins by asking, What is the value of the work which employers and employed are jointly engaged in turning out? If that is valueless or bad, the ethic of workmanship makes this significant affirmation—that no human device, no "system" of one kind or another, can make the relations between the parties to it valuable or good: nothing but thorns and thistles can grow out of that soil. If, on the other hand, the work has value and is good, the ground is then cleared, the soil prepared, and the seed sown for the growth of just and humane relations between the co-operating units, and of all the virtues appropriate to the situation, not excepting pity, mercy and loving-kindness, and whatever else may be counted a passport to eternal life.

Take the case of a great factory run by a limited company for the manufacture of a worthless proprietary article, prospering by advertisement and credulity. The workers shall enjoy the shortest hours and the highest wages you choose to imagine; there shall be profit-sharing and Whitley Councils; there shall be a welfare department and a hospital with trained nurses in constant attendance, a library and a recreation-room—nay, the whole shall be placed, if you will, under government by a proletariat of the workers. What has the ethic of workmanship to say to this? It has to say that the whole affair, welfare department and all, is a demoralising enterprise, in varying degrees, for every human being concerned in it, from the "Chairman of the Directors" to the charwoman. It is a malignant growth in the body of society. And of an industrial civilisation which prospers on those terms, *or is infected by that spirit,* the ethic of workmanship predicts as follows: that it will not *stand,* that its short hours, high wages, "better conditions," and all the rest, will precipitate the downfall of it, that the "right relations" established between the parties to it will end in world-wars and bloody revolutions; for the wall is built with untempered mortar, and, if a "fox go up on it," will collapse. And to those who speak of justice, pity, mercy and loving-kindness as virtues that can be made to flourish in that atmosphere, the ethic of workmanship pays such heed as is due to sounding brass and to tinkling cymbals. Alas! that the ethic of workmanship should have become a Cinderella among the moralities, as indeed it has! Alas! that the ethic of Jesus the Carpenter should have become a New Testament "problem"—of Jesus, who said to the masons, "Raise your stone, and I stand beneath it"; and to His fellow-carpenters, "Split your timber, and I am inside."

Is there none among our legislators and counsellors who, seeing the good that is done by "building a million houses," can see also the harm that is done, the blight that falls on justice, pity, mercy and loving-kindness, by building them—as most houses are built nowadays—with stones that no Christ ever helped in the raising and with timber that he would reject as unsound? What avails it to preach these virtues to the house builder who is laying rotten bricks in untempered mortar? Will he cultivate them, think you, in his "leisure time"? Working all day in the element of the False, the Evil and the Ugly, will he turn in the evening to the True, the Good and the Beautiful? He will not, nor will the age that countenances him. It would seem as though the dishonesty of the jerry builder had infected the very men who would make him honest. What are they, then, but jerry builders themselves? All attempts to find culture, religion, salvation for a working world *outside the sphere of its work* must, from the nature of the matter, resolve themselves ultimately into spoken nothings.

Yet these attempts—to find an effectual culture for a working world *outside* its work— are not to be wondered at. Mechanism, narrowing the scope of our spiritual freedom, has long been driving "conduct" out of work, and what more natural than that we should seek a field for conduct elsewhere? But what other field can we find that will make amends for the one we are losing? This expulsion of "conduct" from work, this reduction of labour to a mechanical operation, with the minimum of scope within it for the exercise of the qualities that make a man, leaving his soul to be cultivated when he is off duty, this, when rightly considered, is the greatest tragedy that could befall industrial civilisation. It must be frankly faced. And in frankly facing it, but not otherwise, it may be that a new form for "conduct" will disclose itself, that, namely, of restoring "conduct" to the sphere where elemental law has planted its roots—which is nothing else than our daily work. A task for giants.

But not insuperable. The means for its accomplishment are actually in being. Just as mercy, pity and loving-kindness have not perished from the earth, but are active in a thousand forms, without self-advertisement, and mostly in ignorance of their own names, so too the tradition of excellent workmanship, and the practice of it, have not to be created anew. Both tradition and practice are to be found everywhere by those who will look for them, waiting to be developed, by right education, into the master-principle of industrial peace and of social and international unity. The fact that they play no part in the programmes of public operators (Labour or other), are unmentioned in the League of Nations, and hardly noticed by professional moralists, who seem to be engaged in a conspiracy to find a field for virtue anywhere but in work, is sufficiently disconcerting; but, in spite of all that, there is still good work enough in the world to hold the fabric of industrial civilisation together and to give promise of better things to come.

It survives, to begin with and chiefly, in the silent heroism of uncounted multitudes who "mind" the vast complex of industrial machinery, doing their work not always, indeed, as well as it might be done, but not so ill as their critics would do it if places were changed. It survives in the excellence of the machinery, which often betrays an almost superhuman skill in the invention of it and a divine thoroughness in the construction of it; a reflection not likely to escape the man of sense who crosses the ocean in a well-found ship, travels from Glasgow to London by the night train, and finds his letters waiting for him next morning—none of which things would be possible had not "the three thousand punctualities" been faithfully observed by multitudes of his fellow-men. It survives in the fiduciary competence, in the trusteeship unbetrayed, of workers in manifold vocations, from the driver of the locomotive to the Chancellor of the Exchequer. These are the forces, these the qualities, which the ethic of workmanship counts on as the growing-point, under right development, of a nobler civilisation than this; claiming thereby affinity with the "Ethic of Jesus" and predicting that many a poor fellow with nothing but a worn shovel to show for himself on the Day of Judgment will find *that* a valid passport into the Kingdom of Heaven—no doubt to his great surprise and to the greater surprise of any pompous professors who may be standing by.

There are other moments, indeed, dark moments of depression, when the ethic of workmanship seems, to the believer in it, to be utterly forsaken and abandoned, a thing on which our civilisation has definitely turned its back with a mind made up to seek its fortunes by other roads—by the introduction of new "systems," by legislative cure-alls, by the incantation of formulæ, by anything but good work. Are not all of us asserting our "right to happiness" and resenting every pang of suffering we have to endure, every renunciation we have to face, as an infraction of that "right" wrought upon us by the universe or by our fellow-men? Are we not all intent on the softest job we can find, the sofest and the best paid, demanding that our work shall be reduced to "four hours a day," so that we may be "happy" for the rest of it, with money in our purses to make all smooth? In an age imbued with these ideas, its fibre softened by them to the last extreme of imbecility and cowardice—so runs the counsel of these dark moments—what chances of a hearing remain for the ethic of workmanship, whose first word is this, that no kind of excellence is possible to man save on condition of *suffering in the achievement of it,* endured by strong souls who scorn to ask themselves whether they are "happy" or not? While the chief wrong a man can inflict on his fellows is held to be that of being "happier" than they are; while the dream of millennialists is of a state where all men are equally "happy"; while churches (foully betraying their thorn-crowned Head), social idealists, political leaders and street agitators are engaged together in fostering this contemptible delusion, all clacking of "happiness" "like a rusty meat-jack" [1]—who, in times so demoralised, can lift up the truth that man is nearer his "rights" when embracing pain than when shirking it, without the certainty that he will be mocked, spat upon and scourged? "All the spiritual ideals of mankind," writes Dr. Felix Adler, "are pang-born." It is profoundly true. But the pangs are not at an end when the ideal is *born*. Greater pangs will have to be endured if the vision of excellence is to become an embodied fact, if the dream of beauty is to be more than an iridescent mist floating ineffectually over an ugly world. The good workman must take up his cross—to no saint or martyr is it more ineluctably assigned than to him. But who in these days of happiness-hunting can persuade us to do *that?*

Such are the questionings, despairs and sad counsels of our darker moments. But they are not final. A deeper scrutiny reveals that the ethic of workmanship still holds its ground, holds it against the poisonous absurdity of "the right to be happy"; that in all "ranks of society" millions of men and women, intent on the work

[1] Carlyle's description of "the unspeakable happiness-philosophy."

in hand, do its behests, undismayed by the call to suffering, unchecked by the thorns that wound them at every step they go. Were this not so, our best-laid schemes for mending the world would come to nothing; statesmen would plough the sand, preachers beat the air, reformers pursue a will-o'-the-wisp. But it is so. All over the world our good workman may be seen on duty, expounding the "ethic" of the business, not in the enticing words of man's wisdom, but in demonstration of the spirit and in power; ploughing, hammering, shovelling, cutting highways through deserts, harnessing cataracts, tunnelling mountains or levelling them into plains; going down to the sea, also, in ships; doing business in great waters, battling with tempests, out-manœuvring the hurricane, watchful in the dark; dexterous, keen-witted, alert; a stout heart on the bridge; a sure eye for the signal; an obedient hand at the wheel. Such is the ethic of workmanship, the Cinderella of the moralists, the forgotten one of the doctrinaires, despised and rejected by the social quacks, the suffering servant of civilisation, standing invisibly between it and ruin, without whose constant vigilance and faithfulness all classes, factions and parties, with their respective "isms" and cure-alls, would find their common level at the bottom of the sea and so make an end of their "right to be happy."

This year we are celebrating the bicentenary of the birth of the great philosopher Emmanuel Kant, born at Königsberg in 1724. Behind the other questions which Kant set out to answer, and summarising them all, lay the question of the rich young ruler, "What shall I do to inherit eternal life?—how shall I win the unconditional good?" Kant's answer is contained in the well-known maxim, "Do thy duty for thy duty's sake." In this maxim his entire philosophy comes to the point: all the rest is preparatory to that. Except through the gateway of duty done for duty's sake he saw no practicable opening into the realm of the unconditionally *good*, which is the realm of eternal life. To which the ethic of workmanship replies, "Amen, so be it!"

But what is "our duty," and where does it lie? In answer to that the ethic of workmanship affirms that, for an industrial age, the main field of duty is the field of *industry*. To the potter standing at his wheel our ethic says, "Your main duty in this universe is to make the best pot you can. If you wilfully make your pot evil, nothing that you can achieve in other departments will make *you* an acceptable potter, and the gates of eternal life will be barred to you."

And if, as is likely, your wheel is one of a thousand driven from a central power-house, with little control over the pot left to *you,* the ethic of workmanship exhorts you to stand to it manfully nevertheless, and do the best you can within your limits, promising meanwhile to fight a battle on your behalf, with you as an enlisted soldier, against principalities and powers, until the public has been trained to buy no pots, and manufacturers to make none, save just such pots as have educated the potter and made a man of him. Your lot is hard; but so is that of those who fight with you and for you. You have other counsellors, no doubt; but they no more than we can deliver you off-hand from the limitations of your work; they no more than we can break the tyranny of the power-house by a *coup de main:* which is the evil that remains to you when all others are gone. By-and-by the power-house itself shall be converted and the public come over to your side; doubt it not; nay, is being converted, is coming over to your side, slowly but surely, at this very hour. Look at the pots in yonder shop window and compare them with the pots your grandmother used to buy. What do you see? You see *better pots*. *Laus Deo!* The battle shall yet be won, and you, who have stood to it manfully in the meantime, doing the best you can within your limitations, shall be a building stone of the city that hath foundations.

> "For that city we must *labour*,
>   For its sake bear pain and grief,
> In it find the end of living,
>   And the anchor of belief."

Needless to say, the potter our ethic has in mind is industrial society considered both as a single working unit and as a multitude of such; the wheel at which he stands is the entire complex of social mechanism both ponderable and imponderable; and the pot is the sum-total of goods and services turned out from day to day. To make all that as good, true and beautiful as human skill and faithfulness can make it, is the summary *duty* of industrial civilisation as understood by the ethic of workmanship; which duty neglected, or lightly passed by, that civilisation will remain barred out from its spiritual inheritance, as an undutiful servant, justly afflicted with miseries and degradations, in spite of all that the schools, universities, Churches and Labour Governments can effect to the contrary. In this way the ethic of workmanship carries on the tradition of Emmanuel Kant, sharpening his doctrine of duty for duty's sake, which he left blunt, to a spear-head, and seeking thereby to pierce an opening for a revival of religion and of the fine arts—of which fine arts, as was said before, the art of righteous living is the consummation. For the chief product of the potter's wheel is always the potter himself.

It is on the ethic of workmanship, so understood, that hope now centres as the only means discernible for bridging the fatal gulf, created by mass production, between the work that "fills our bellies" and the culture that "saves our souls." The way is arduous and long; but longer and more arduous roads have been trodden before, and we must not despair. The ethic of workmanship does not look for quick results.

It has no magic formula for creating the millennium. It has neither pills nor potions.

The time will be long before professional moralists recognise the inadequacy of suburban operations. It will be long before the builders of the New Jerusalem have learnt the difference between spinning cobwebs and laying foundations. It will be long before the general public, misled by a discredited philosophy, can be brought to believe that "the pursuit of happiness" is the most paltry of all the undertakings to which man could engage himself and a prime cause of his miseries. It will be long before statesmen and educationists co-operate effectively in "transfiguring the work of the world from a burden that crushes into a culture that ennobles mankind." Yet the ethic of workmanship aims at nothing less than all this, and will not rest until it be accomplished. The end is clear: the steps that lead to it are not clear. And will not be, until multitudes of ingenious minds, grasping the main principle, have pooled their resources for discovering the steps. Then miracles will begin to happen. The ethic of workmanship contemplates creative work; but its own creation is, as yet, but half complete, like that of the lion in *Paradise Lost:*

> "now half appeared
> The tawny lion, pawing to get free
> His hinder parts; then springs, as broke from bonds,
> And rampant shakes his brinded mane."

THE END